LAURIE LEE

TO WAR IN SPAIN

PENGUIN BOOKS

PENGUIN BOOKS

Published by the Penguin Group. Penguin Books Ltd, 27 Wrights Lane, London W8 5TZ, England. Penguin Books USA Inc., 375 Hudson Street, New York, New York 10014, USA. Penguin Books Australia Ltd, Ringwood, Victoria, Australia. Penguin Books Canada Ltd, 10 Alcorn Avenue, Toronto, Ontario, Canada M4V 3B2. Penguin Books (NZ) Ltd, 182–190 Wairau Road, Auckland 10, New Zealand · Penguin Books Ltd, Registered Offices: Harmondsworth, Middlesex, England · The first extract is from *As I Walked Out One Midsummer Morning,* by Laurie Lee, first published by André Deutsch 1969. Published in Penguin Books 1971. The second extract is from *A Moment of War*, by Laurie Lee, first published by Viking 1991. Published in Penguin Books 1992. This edition published 1996. · Typeset by Rowland Phototypesetting Ltd, Bury St Edmunds, Suffolk. Printed in England by Clays Ltd, St Ives plc · · 10 9 8 7 6 5 4 3 2 1

To War in Spain

I

Plucked from the Civil War by a British destroyer, I returned to my Gloucestershire village, amazed to see once more the depth of the grass and the weight of the leaves on the trees. But the pleasure of being home again, and receiving the traditional cosseting of the prodigal, was quickly replaced by misgivings. I'd been away two years, but was little the wiser for it. I was twenty-two, woolly-minded, and still naïve in everything, but I began to realize I'd come home too soon.

The Spanish War, seen close to within the local limits of an Andalusian village, was not what it had seemed to me at the time. As I learnt more about it from the newspapers – its scale and implications – I couldn't help feeling a private sense of betrayal.

Unlike so many of my age, for whom Spain in the Thirties represented one of the last theatres of political romanticism, I hadn't consciously chosen it as a Cause but had stumbled on it by accident, simply by happening to be there. Now I began to feel shameful doubts at having turned my back on events so easily, just when they were about to affect us all. I thought the least I could do was to give myself a second chance by returning to Spain as soon as I could.

It was a restless summer. I was penniless, without contacts, and totally ignorant of ways and means. Spain was over a thousand miles away and already sealed off by the hypocrisies of non-intervention. I might have given up the idea if I hadn't suddenly fallen in love, but the result of that experience, which went deeper than anything I'd known before, only made my situation all the more intolerable.

For me it was an hallucination of honour, no doubt a self-indulgence, irrelevant to events and certainly irrelevant to the girl. I told her my plans one evening as she sat twisting her hair with her fingers and gazing into my eyes with her long cat look. She wasn't impressed. Others may need a war, she said; but you don't, you've got one here. She bared her beautiful small teeth and unsheathed her claws. Heroics like mine didn't mean a thing. If I wished to command her admiration by sacrificing myself to a cause she herself was ready to provide one.

Of course, I tried to persuade her that I would be doing it for her, but this wasn't true, and she knew it. All the same, it was partly our entanglement that drove me, the feeling of over-indulgence and satiety brought on by too much easy and unearned pleasure. Guilt, too: she was married and had two young children, she was rich and demandingly beautiful, extravagantly generous with her emotions but fanatically jealous, and one who gave more than she got in love. For several days and nights our arguments swung back and forth, interspersed with desperate embraces, ending with threats of blackmail and bitter tears, with cries of 'Go, and you'll see me no more . . .'

With the help of another friend, I left London in the autumn and worked my way down through France, heading in the direction of the Pyrenees, planning, when the chances were right, simply to walk into the mountains and slip across the frontier alone. The Pyrenees, when I got there, were already touched with snow and looked grey and impregnable. Even so, I never doubted that I could get across. Winter was closing in like a cloak.

While I was waiting near the coast and making some rather slip-shod preparations, the girl suddenly turned up again, having driven out from England not in an attempt to dissuade me further but to present me instead with a week of passionate farewell. A week of hysteria, too – embracing in ruined huts, on the salt-grass at the edge of the sea, gazing out at the windswept ocean while gigantic thunderstorms wheeled slowly round the distant mountains.

There were no more questions or arguments; the mountains were always in sight, and the girl made it clear she thought I was going to my death. Our love was more violent than ever, as though we accepted this as its end and wished to leave each other destroyed.

After we parted, I moved on to the little town of Perpignan, only about twelve miles from the Pyrenees. Perpignan, I'd been told, was swarming with Spanish Government agents eager to recruit volunteers and smuggle them over the mountains. Certainly the agents were there, but they must have thought me a doubtful proposition for my approaches were either blocked or met by evasions. When I mentioned the

International Brigade, the Spanish Consul was polite and said he had no knowledge of such a body. He appreciated my goodwill but assured me that he ran no excursions across the frontier: such junketings would be unthinkable and lawless. The war was a domestic matter, he said, and everything was going well; but if I really wished to help I should go back home.

I spent a couple of weeks in the town without breaking through this wall of equivocation, and finally I realized I would have to go it alone. The Pyrenees to the south, seen in the sharp winter air, began to look smaller and less non-committal. So early in December I took a bus to Ceret in the foothills, where I spent my last snug night in an inn. Then next morning, at first light, I left the still sleeping village and started off up the mountain track.

Behind me, as I climbed, the gentle slopes of the foothills fell away to Perpignan and the sea, while before me the steep bulk of the

Pyrenees Orientales filled the sky with their sunlit peaks. I had about eight hours of daylight but was not too sure of my route, except that it must go up, over, and south. The fact that it was winter seemed to be the only thing in my favour, though I was still glad of the bright clear weather.

The track rose steeply among rocks that were diamond-crusted with ice, and I soon found the going tough. I was idiotically equipped for such a journey, having brought nothing that would help me, though plenty of stuff that wouldn't – no maps, no compass, no tent or ground-sheet, instead a rucksack loaded down with an assortment of books and papers, together with my violin, a folding camera, and a saucepan. I don't really know why I was carrying all this, except that it was all I had in the world.

Throughout the long clear morning I struggled up the mountain path, buffeted by icy winds from the north. The great peak of

Canigou stood away on my right, floating in the brilliant sky like an iceberg, and for much of the time, not having a compass, I was able to use it as a sighting post. By noon I'd climbed to about 3,000 feet, but the goat track grew more and more tortuous, so I decided to abandon it altogether and go straight up the mountain, still keeping Canigou on my right.

The way was tricky and hard, and I found myself stumbling on my knees and clawing at rock and tufts of frozen grass. By the middle of the afternoon I was sweating in the cold, slipping and scrambling over the broken slopes. But I was high up now, with a prickling across the back of my neck as I felt the whole of France plunging away behind me. Having been born and brought up at two hundred and fifty feet above sea-level, I was not used to such dizzying elevations.

Suddenly there was an ominous change in the atmosphere, an extra keenness of cold, and a curious glare and whitening of the sunlight. Looking down, I saw that the foothills had disappeared and had been replaced by a blanket of swirling vapour. The shining peak of Canigou began to switch on and off like a lighthouse, intermittently shuttered by racing clouds. Then the wind rose abruptly to a thin-edged wail, and I felt the first stinging bite of snow.

One moment I'd been climbing a mountain in a sparkle of sunshine; the next, the whole visible world had gone, and I was slapped to my knees and pinioned to a shelf of rock, head down in a driving gale. Gusts of snow swept round me, needling into my eyelids and piercing my clothes like powdered glass. The storm closed in and began scouring the mountain with an insane and relentless frenzy.

For a while I curled myself up and became just a ball of survival, mindlessly hugging the lee of a rock. I lay knee to chin, letting the storm ride over me; then I began to wonder what I was doing here. After all the boasting I'd done in summer fields back home, and in her Chanel-scented bed, what was I doing in France stuck to the face of a mountain alone in a winter blizzard? To lie freezing to death on the wrong side of the frontier was no way to go to a war. There was no point in staying where I was, so I started to move forward, crawling slowly on hands and knees. Distance, direction, movement, and balance were all fused by the driving snow; I may have advanced half a mile, or just a few yards, there was no longer any way of knowing. All I remember is the brightness of the ground, and being swept by waves of almost infantile pleasure, the delirious warmth of impending frostbite.

Then, by one of those long-shot chances, taken for granted at the time, I came upon a rough little stone-built shelter. It was half in ruins, and there was nothing inside it but straw, but I suppose it may have saved my life. Once

I'd bedded myself down, I heard the blizzard change gear, rising to an almost supersonic shriek, and for a couple of hours I lay motionless, curled deep in the straw, slowly and painfully thawing out.

Later it grew dark, and the anguish gradually eased as I built up a drowsy fug for myself. The sound of the wind settled down to a steady whine, soporific, like an electric motor. A pleasant comfort crept over me; I seemed to sense the feathersoft snow gathering in deep weightless drifts outside; a bosomy presence, invisible and reassuring, cushioning the naked rocks of the mountain. By now I was exhausted anyway, too drugged by the cold to move, even to attempt to build a fire; so I just lay, sniffing the damp warm smell of the straw, and presently I fell asleep.

Next morning the storm was over and the sun shone brilliantly again. I came out of the dark little hut to find the mountain transformed –

trees, rocks, and bushes thickly bolstered with snow and giving off a clean crispy smell, like starch. The French village below me was no longer in sight, but the slope above curved gradually away, smooth and bright, rising a few hundred yards then ending in a sharp blue line of sky.

Abandoning the cosy gully where I'd spent the night, I climbed unsteadily for an hour or so, ploughing through snowdrifts, stumbling over hidden rocks, and slithering about in my sodden shoes. It was a long cold struggle, and I'd had nothing to eat, but at least I was lucky to be on the move at all. Then suddenly there was no more climbing: the slope levelled and stopped, the sky plunged, and I was on top of the ridge.

The icy crests of the Pyrenees stretched east and west, flashing in the sun like broken glass on a wall, while before me, to the south, was
 what I had come to see – range after range of

little step-like hills falling away to the immensities of Spain . . .

But I was not over the mountains yet; there was still another ridge to cross, with a deep valley lying between. I could see a black frozen stream winding a thousand feet below me. I would simply have to go down and up again.

Crossing this mile-wide chasm took me the rest of the day – a vertical, trackless journey. Whipped by flurries of snow and bruising winds I slithered, slipped, and scrambled, seeing no living thing except a boy and a sheepdog who both fled when they saw me coming. Towards evening, very cold, and with a rime of frost on my eyelashes, I was about half-way up the second slope, when I came to a small mountain road, the first I'd seen for two days, winding bleakly among the trees. I sat and stared at it for a while, but it told me nothing; it could have been anywhere on earth - just an inscrutable little cart-track, half mud, half stones, as nameless as a peasant's face.

But darkness was coming now, and I was limp with hunger. I didn't fancy another night on the mountain. So I thought I'd better follow the road and see where it led me, even if it meant a clash with the frontier guards. The track wound upwards for half a mile through a thicket of pine trees and presently emerged in a little clearing. I saw roof-tops, a church, and a cluster of village lights. Then I smelt hot butter, and knew I was still in France.

Except for a hobbled horse and a couple of snarling dogs, the village street was empty. The low wooden houses, crudely thatched with bracken, had a look of dark Siberian squalor; but half-way up the street I saw the lights of a café shining warmly through steamed-up windows. I pushed open the door and entered

 a noisy room full of little men in sheep's-wool

coats. But when they saw me they froze as though I'd let in a blast of snow, and their conversation switched off abruptly.

What rough beast was this slouching towards the bar, dressed in a blanket and crumpled hat, coming out of the night like some ghost of winter, his hair and eyebrows white with frost? Nobody moved or spoke, except the old woman behind the bar who bobbed quickly out of sight as I approached her, and whose place was immediately taken by a huge-bellied man who began setting up bottles like a defensive wall.

I asked if I could have something to eat, and he repeated the question to the room, then, after a pause, nodded to an empty table. I slumped down in the chair, and presently he brought me some soup, which seemed to be a mixture of tar and onions. As I ate, the men watched me – rows of bright little faces wrapped to the ears in their fleece-lined collars. Some quietly shuffled their dominoes, others winked cryptically at one another, all seemed to be waiting for something to happen.

At last a committee of three detached themselves from the rest and came over and sat at my table. They were low-voiced and confidential, and one of them offered me a cigarette. I didn't have to answer, but they'd rather like to know: what exactly was I doing here? I'd come from Perpignan, hadn't I? I'd been seen there several times recently; also down in Ceret, a couple of days ago. It was hard on the mountain at this time of the year. I mustn't mind their curiosity.

They were a strange little trio but seemed harmless enough. One of them wore the look of a sleepy clown; the other had a Karl Marx beard, extravagantly bushy and white; the third was thin, like a weathered pole. But the warmth of the room, the soup, and their polite concern encouraged me to take a chance. I told them I

 was on my way to the 'south'. I had friends

there, I said – I wanted to join them, that was all. They asked a few more questions, then the fat clown smiled. 'Well, since you've got this far . . .' he said. He called for some brandy and poured me a glass. 'Drink it up, man. You're going to need it.'

I was lucky. It might just as easily have gone the other way, with an ignominious return to Perpignan. But it seemed I'd fallen on my feet among the very men who could help me: a cosy community of frontier anarchists. I don't know why they decided to trust me, or why they thought me worth the trouble, but clearly they'd made up their minds. The men put their heads together and held a brief discussion, then the thin one looked at his watch and nodded. 'It'll take us an hour,' he said, 'so as soon as you're ready. Better go before the moon comes up.'

He rose to his feet and wrapped a scarf round his long thin neck as though he was lagging a water pipe. The others helped me on with my bags and I was given some more brandy for the journey. The proprietor refused to be paid for the soup. Then the thin man said ‘Come’, and pushed open the door to admit a flurry of powdered snow, and we left the café to a murmur of benevolent farewells and a flourish of political salutes.

Once in the street, my companion glanced quickly at the sky, put out his cigarette, and rolled up his collar. ‘Stay close, and say nothing,’ he muttered briefly, then shot off up a narrow lane. I hurried after him, and we were out of the village immediately, climbing a steep and brutish path. The man raced on ahead of me, taking little goat-like leaps and dodging nimbly from rock to rock. I could see his tall gaunt figure bouncing against the hazy stars. He never bothered to check that I was still behind him.

Easy enough for him, I thought: he was built

for these mountains while I'd been raised on very low hills. His legs were long and mine were short – I was also carrying a twenty-pound load. I did my best to keep with him but he soon outstripped me and I started to fall farther and farther back. I wanted to shout, 'Wait a minute!' but it didn't seem to be the thing to do. Instead, I began to indulge in a bit of carefree whistling.

That stopped him in the end. I found him perched on a rock waiting impatiently for me to catch up. 'Stop whistling,' he growled. 'Save it for the other side. This is no time for trivialities.' At least I was grateful for the halt, and the conversation. I asked him if he did this often. I must be mad, he said; it was the very first time, and by God he was sorry already.

He started climbing again while I went panting behind him, sweat trickling down my arms and legs. Brittle gusts of dry snow swept by on the wind, striking the face like handfuls of rice.

I felt engulfed by a contest that was growing too large for me; something I'd asked for but doubted that I could carry through. My companion ignored this, pushing ahead more relentlessly than ever, as though wishing to put me to the final test. That last half-hour was perhaps the worst I've known, casually unprepared as I was; ill-shod, badly clothed, and lumbered with junk, clawing my way up these icy slopes.

The point of collapse must have been near, but luckily I escaped it, for at last we reached the top of the rise. We were in a narrow pass flanked by slabs of rock which stood metallic and blue in the starlight. I seemed to sense a change in the air, a curious lifting of pressure before me as though some great obstacle had been rolled away. There was also a faint smell of charcoal, woodsmoke, and mules, and an indefinable whiff of pepper. My guide drew me into the shadows and gestured me to silence, sticking out his neck and sniffing the sky. We crouched in the darkness listening. We heard the wind, falling water, and what sounded like a distant gunshot.

'This is where I leave you,' said the Frenchman. He appeared a little more cheerful now. 'The frontier is between those rocks. Follow the path for half a kilometre and you'll come to a little farm. Knock on the door and you'll be among your friends.'

Suddenly it seemed too simple – after weeks of speculation and doubt, and these last two exhausting days – just a gap in the rocks a few hundred yards ahead of me, the tiny frontier between peace and war.

'Move slow and easy. There may be a few guards about but they shouldn't be too lively on a night like this. If you're challenged, drop everything and run like hell. Good luck, then; I can do no more.'

But there was no opposition. I just walked

towards the rocks and slipped between them as though on an evening stroll. A narrow path led downwards among the boulders. Then, after about half a kilometre, just as the Frenchman had said, I saw a little farmhouse and knocked on the door. It was opened by a young man with a rifle who held up a lantern to my face. I noticed he was wearing the Republican armband.

'I've come to join you,' I said.

'*Pase usted*,' he answered.

I was back in Spain, with a winter of war before me.

II

The young man slung his rifle over his shoulder and motioned me to enter the hut. A dark passage led to a smoky room. Inside, in a group, stood an old man and woman, another youth with a gun, and a gaunt little girl about eleven years old. They were huddled together like a family photograph fixing me with glassy teeth-set smiles. There was a motionless silence while they took me in – seeing a young tattered stranger, coatless and soaked to the knees, carrying a kit-bag from which a violin bow protruded. Suddenly the old woman said 'Ay!' and beckoned me to the fire, which was piled high with glowing pine cones.

I crouched, thawing out by the choking fumes, sensing deeply this moment of arrival.

I felt it first when threading through the high rocks of the frontier, when, almost by pressures in the atmosphere, and the changes of sound and scent, a great door seemed to close behind me, shutting off entirely the country I'd left; and then, as the southern Pyrenees fell away at my feet, this new one opened, with a rush of raw air, admitting all the scarred differences and immensities of Spain. At my back was the tang of Gauloises and slumberous sauces, scented flesh and opulent farmlands; before me, still ghostly, was all I remembered – the whiff of rags and woodsmoke, the salt of dried fish, sour wine and sickness, stone and thorn, old horses and rotting leather.

'Will you eat?' asked the woman.

'Don't be mad,' said her husband.

He cleared part of the table, and the old woman gave me a spoon and a plate. At the other end the little girl was cleaning a gun, frowning, tongue out, as though doing her homework. An old black cooking-pot hung over the smouldering pine cones, from which the woman ladled me out some soup. It was hot, though thin, a watery mystery that might have been the tenth boiling of the bones of a hare. As I ate, my clothes steaming, shivering and warming up, the boys knelt by the doorway, hugging their rifles and watching me. Everybody watched me except for the gun-cleaning girl who was intent on more urgent matters. But I could not, from my appearance, offer much of a threat, save for the mysterious bundle I carried. Even so, the first suspicious silence ended; a light joky whispering seemed to fill the room.

'What are you?'

'I'm English.'

'Ah, yes – he's English.'

They nodded to each other with grave politeness.

'And how did you come here perhaps?'

'I came over the mountain.'

'Yes, he walked over the mountain . . . on foot.'

They were all round me at the table now as I ate my soup, all pulling at their eyes and winking, nodding delightedly and repeating everything I said, as though humouring a child just learning to speak.

'He's come to join us,' said one of the youths; and that set them off again, and even the girl lifted her gaunt head and simpered. But I was pleased too, pleased that I managed to get here so easily after two days' wandering among peaks and blizzards. I was here now with friends. Behind me was peace-engorged France. The people in the kitchen were a people stripped for war – the men smoking beech leaves, the soup reduced to near water; around us hand-grenades hanging on the walls like strings of onions; muskets and cartridge-belts piled in the corner, and open orange-boxes packed with silver bullets like fish. War was still so local then, it was like stepping into another room. And this was what I had come to re-visit. But I was now awash with sleep, hearing the blurred murmuring of voices and feeling the rocks of Spain under my feet. The men's eyes grew narrower, watching the unexpected stranger, and his lumpy belongings drying by the fire. Then the old woman came and took me by the elbow and led me upstairs and one of the boys followed close behind. I was shown into a small windowless room of bare white-washed stone containing a large iron bed smothered with goatskins. I lay down exhausted, and the old woman put an oil lamp on the floor, placed a cold hand on my brow, and left me with a gruff good-night. The room had no door, just an opening in the wall, and the boy stretched himself languidly across the threshold. He lay on his side, his chin resting on the stock of his gun, watching me with large black unblinking eyes. As I slipped into sleep I remembered I had left all my baggage downstairs; but it didn't seem to matter now.

I was awoken early next morning by the two armed brothers who were dressed for outdoors in ponchos of rabbit skin. They gave me a bucket of snow to wash in, then led me gingerly downstairs and sat me on a stool where the old lady poured me some coffee. The little girl, her hair brushed and shining already, was fitting ammunition into cartridge-belts. As I drank my coffee – which tasted of rusty buttons – she looked at me with radiant shyness.

'He came over the mountains,' she said perkily, nodding to herself.

The boys giggled, and the old man coughed.

They brought me my baggage and helped me sling it over my shoulders, and told me that a horse and cart were waiting for me outside.

'They sent it up from the town specially.

 They didn't want to keep you hanging about

. . . Well, not after you came all that way to join us.'

The boys half-marched me into the lane and the rest of the family followed and stood watching, blowing on their purple fingers. The old woman and child had bright shawls on their heads, while, for some reason, the old man wore a tall top hat.

The cart waiting in the lane resembled a rough-looking tumbril, and the driver had a cavernous, nervous face. 'Vamanos, vamanos, vamanos,' he kept muttering plaintively, giving me glances of sharp distaste.

The boys helped me into the back of the cart and climbed up after me.

'Here he is. The English one,' they said with ponderous jocularity.

The driver sniffed, and uncoiled his whip.

'Horse and cart,' said one of the brothers, nudging me smartly. 'We've got to save your legs. They must be half destroyed with all this walking over mountains. And what have we got if we haven't got your legs? You wouldn't be much use to us, would you?'

I was beginning to get a bit bored with all this levity, and sat there silent and shivering. The boys perched close beside me, one on each side, holding their guns at the ready, like sentries. Every so often they pointed them at me and nodded brightly. They appeared to be in a state of nervous high spirits. 'Vamanos!' snarled the driver, and shook up the reins crossly. The old man and his wife raised their hands solemnly and told me to go with God. The little girl threw a stone at the horse, or it may have been at me, but it hit the horse and caused it to start with a jerk. So we began to lumber and creak down the steep rocky lane, the brothers now holding me by either elbow. The Pyrenees stood high behind us, white and hard, their peaks colouring to the rising sun.
 The boys nodded towards them, grinning,

nudging me sharply again, and baring their chestnut-tinted teeth.

Through the iced winter morning, slipping over glassy rocks, we made our stumbling way down the valley, passing snow-covered villages, empty and bare, from which all life and sound seemed withdrawn. This chilling silence was surely not one of nature, which could be broken by a goat-bell or the chirp of a bird. It was as if a paralysing pestilence had visited the place, and I was to notice it on a number of occasions in the weeks to come. It was simply the stupefying numbness of war.

After an hour or so we came to a small hill town still shuttered by the shadow of rocks. A bent woman crept by, bearing a great load of firewood. A cat shot through a hole in a wall. I noticed that the brothers had suddenly grown tense and anxious, sitting straight as pillars, thin-lipped, beside me. Two militiamen, in khaki ponchos, came out of a doorway and marched ahead of us down the street. Even our driver perked up and began to look around him with what appeared to be an air of importance. The militiamen led us into the square, to the dilapidated Town Hall, from which the Republican flag was hanging. The brothers called out to a couple of sentries who were sitting on the steps, and one of them got up and went inside. Now for a proper welcome, I thought. I got down from the cart, and the brothers followed. Then four soldiers came out with fixed bayonets.

'We've brought you the spy,' said the brothers, and pushed me forward. The soldiers closed round me and handcuffed my wrists.

They put me in a cellar and left me for two days. I got a kind of soup the first day, and they forgot me the next – waiting and forgetting being just another part of the war. It was damp and very cold, the walls of the cellar limed with ice like spidery veins of lace. But luckily I'd been toughened up by the cottage bedrooms of home where the water in wash-basins froze solid in winter. The cell had a curious, narrow, coffin-like shape, and even had iron rings round the walls as though to lift it up from inside. There was one dim, yellow-coloured light-bulb hanging from the ceiling, but no furniture; I slept on the rocky floor.

Lying there, shivering, unvisited, well on into the third day, I was wondering idly what now might happen. This was not, after all, quite what I had expected. I had walked into a country at war uninvited and unannounced, and had found no comradely welcome, only suspicion and silence. I am surprised now how little surprised I was then, but I was soon to learn how natural this was.

Captain Perez was again not what I'd expected. He came for me in the late afternoon of the third day, opening my cellar door with a light whispering key. No whiskered revolutionary he, but a slim tailored dandy, a smart gleaming figure in elegantly belted uniform, and with riding boots so glazed and polished his legs appeared to be chocolate-coated. He smiled at me from the doorway, and held out a tin mug of coffee.

'Are you rested?' he asked, in a soft furry voice.

I took the coffee and drank it, hunched up on the floor, while he fetched in two chairs and placed them facing each other.

'Please sit down,' he said gently. 'Or, rather, stand up and sit down.' And he gave a sharp little affected laugh.

The officer seemed to have sleepy eyes and a lazy manner, but once seated in front of me his attitude became abrupt and clinical. How, where and why had I come to Spain? When I told him, he shook his head sadly.

'No, señor! Not over the Pyrenees. Not with

all that circus equipment you were carrying. Books, cameras – and a violin, dear Jesus.' He laid a delicate warm hand on my knee. 'You know what we think, young friend? Not over the mountains – no. You came from the sea. You were landed by boat or submarine. From Bremen, was it? You mustn't be surprised that we know all this. We even know what you've come to do.'

He smiled with cream-faced satisfaction, shaking his head against my denials and explanations, and giving my knee another squeeze.

'But, comrade,' I said.

'Captain Perez,' he corrected.

'If you don't believe me, you've got my passport.'

'We've got dozens, dear boy. All of them phonies. And we've got an office that turns out twenty a day.' He looked at me solemnly. 'It was the violin that did it. And the German accent. You would never fool anyone, you know.'

He rose and went to the door, and clapped his hands. There was a heavy marching of feet. The four guards I'd seen earlier came tumbling into the cellar, so wrapped up there was scarcely space for the lot of us. But they circled me close in a friendly manner, trying to keep their bayonets out of each other's eyes.

'Go with them,' said the officer. 'They'll look after you.' And he stepped back into the passage to make room. As we went past him, he snapped a salute in farewell – shining, oiled and immaculate, the last of his kind I was to see in that war.

The guards marched me out into the courtyard and it was night already, with a freezing moon in the sky. The town was empty and silent, dark and shuttered, not even a child or dog could be heard. My guards clumped beside me,

 jogging me along by the elbows, relaxed now,

puffing and whistling. They were all rather short, like Tartars; vapour billowed from their nostrils. The shortest one spun his rifle and grinned up in my face. 'Well,' he said. 'You come a long way to see us. Over the mountains? That's what we hear.' 'That's right,' I said. 'Well, we're nearly there,' he said. 'You won't have to march around much longer.'

Truly we didn't go far – down a short alley and into a rough moonlit scrapyard – till we came to a hole in the ground. The men cleared the snow round the edge, and raised a metal cover, and into the dark cavity they dropped me. It was not very deep – about six to eight feet, narrow, and walled with rock. 'Good-night, Rubio,' they called. 'Warmer down there than on the mountain tops. In this weather, you understand?' They lowered the iron cover over my head and secured it with heavy bolts. Then I heard them stamping away in the snow, and I was alone again.

The hole was wider at the bottom than at the top, and I curled up on some damp, mouldy straw. The darkness was absolute; I couldn't even see the stars through the grille. Drawing up my knees to my chin, and blowing on my fingers, I now began to consider my position. I was still not altogether surprised at what was happening to me. Indeed, I was letting it happen without question or protest. But since my arrival in Spain something quite unexpected had taken over, and I don't think I realized at that stage how sinister it might be, or what grave peril I had got myself into.

I knew I was not the only one to have wandered over the frontier to join the Republicans. There must have been other volunteers who arrived alone – but were they then always dropped into dark little holes like this? Could it be some sort of discipline to test us out, to prove our loyalty of mind?

 I was cold and hungry now, and in this black

icy silence I began to get a sharpening taste of danger. No, thought I, this was clearly not a normal reception. The first two shivering days in the Town Hall cell may simply have been a matter of form. But then to have been cast headlong into this medieval pit seemed to suggest that I'd been picked out for something special.

But still my situation didn't disturb me too much, but rather injected me with a sharp sting of adventure. I was at that flush of youth which never doubts self-survival, that idiot belief in luck and a uniquely charmed life, without which illusion few wars would be possible. I felt the seal of fate on me, and a certain grim intoxication, alone in this buried silence. But macabre as things were, I had no idea then how very near to death I was . . .

It may have been a couple of days, or but a few hours, later that I heard the shuffle of returning feet overhead. The iron cover was removed; I saw a brief flash of stars, and another prisoner was dropped into the hole beside me. 'Now you've got a committee!' a voice called down, and the cover was lowered and bolted and the shuffling feet went away.

We stood close together in the darkness, each other's prisoner now, and twin gaolers, in this tomb of rock. 'They sent this for you,' he said, and his hands found me blindly, and I took the hard piece of broken bread. There was just room for both of us if we lay down together; I couldn't see him but at least the air grew warmer. For about a week we shared this black cave together, visited only at night by the guards overhead, who unbolted the manhole and briefly raised it while they lowered us bread, watered wine, and a bucket.

Strange being huddled so close and for so long to another human being whose face one was unable to see. I knew him to be young by

 his voice and breath and the chance touch of

his hand when sharing food or wine. He also had a fresh wild smell about him, an outdoor smell, a mixture of pine and olives. I remember we slept a good deal, prey to an extraordinary lassitude, and, in the intervals, we talked. He was a deserter, he said; and seemed quite cheerful about it, laughing at the looking-glass differences between us. I was trying to get into the war, and he was trying to get out of it, and here we were, stuffed into the same black hole. I'd come over the mountains from France, and he'd been caught going the other way, and most certainly now, he said, we'd both be shot.

And why not, indeed? The deserter appeared quite fatalistic about it. Patiently, drowsily, with no complaint or self-pity, my companion explained the situation to me. The Civil War was eighteen months old, and entering a bitter winter. The Republican forces were in retreat and could afford to take no chances. Franco's rebels were better armed, and had powerful allies abroad, while our side had few weapons, few friends, almost no food, and had learned to trust no one but the dead. What could you expect them to do with a couple of doubtful characters like us? They couldn't afford to keep us, feed us, or even turn us loose. Even less could they afford the luxury of a trial. So it was thought safer, and quicker, that anyone under suspicion be shot, and this was being done regretfully as a matter of course.

My companion was called Dino, he said, and he was twenty-two years old, and he came from a little village in the Guadarramas. When his village had been burned by the Moors, in the early days, he'd run with his younger brother through the lines and become a dynamiter. They'd worked alone, and he'd seen his brother blown up when some of the fuses went wrong. He'd fought at Guadalajara, but didn't like that kind of warfare – mostly hanging about in ditches, then massacre and panic – so he'd taken off again and headed north for France. He'd been picked up twice, and had twice got away, but he reckoned they'd collared him now for good. He knew what to expect, yes sir. He'd seen quite a number of prisoners and deserters shot, and spoke of the Republicans' methods of execution – casual, informal, often good-humoured. Locked in the dark with Dino, and listening to him describe these scenes in his soft, joky voice, I drew steadily, as I thought, towards my hour, and wondered which of the two of us would be called out first.

When it came, it came suddenly, with us both half-asleep, the iron trap-door above raised with a swift muted action, and a low voice calling the young deserter's name, giving us just time enough for a quick fumbling handshake.

As they raised Dino towards the opening he lifted his arms, and I saw his face in a brief glimmer of moonlight. It was thin and hollow, his eyes huge and glowing, his long pointed countenance like an El Greco saint ascending. Finally two dark shapes pulled him through the narrow entrance, and the manhole was lowered again. I heard the clink of glasses, some moments of casual chatter, Dino's short laugh, then a pistol shot . . .

I'd been standing propped against the wall and listening, and now that it was over I slumped back on the straw. My hand touched the deserter's forage-cap, which he'd left behind. It was damp with sweat and still warm from his head.

A few days later, in the red light of dawn, the grille was dragged open and a voice called, 'Hey, Rubio! . . .' Arms reached down to help me, hands caught my wrists, and I was lifted bodily out of the sepulchre.

My legs were shaking, but I put this down

to two weeks without exercise; and the dawn light stung my eyes. Was it my turn now? The courtyard glittered with snow; and the hurried preparations which I'd expected – the chair, the hand-cart, the plain wooden box, the sleepy officer with the bottle of coñac, the ragged soldiers lined up and looking at their feet – all were present. But not for me. Another young man sat bound to the chair, smoking furiously and chattering like a parrot.

But I was guided quickly across the yard and out into the lane, where two armed guards stood waiting beside a black battered car. They pushed me into the back seat and sat one on each side of me. A broad man in a hat sat up in front by the driver.

We drove fast and silently through the hunched unhappy town and out into the empty country. We climbed a poor bumpy road on to a desolate plateau across which the wind swept pink ruffles of snow. A plateau of scattered rock and thorn, and a few bent bushes, and the wide winter sky closing in.

It became hot and airless in the car, and the guards, in their heavy brown overcoats, began to steam like sweating horses. Their nostrils steamed too, and their noses shone, and dripped on the bayonets held between their knees.

They were an odd-looking couple, the guards – one small and clownlike, with bright blue chin, the other pink and chubby, a mother's boy. I tried to talk to them, but they wouldn't answer; though one whistled knowingly between his teeth. We drove fast, swaying together on the curves, along a road that was both empty and drear.

Where were we going, and what was in store for me? In spite of the guards' silence, I felt I knew this already. Something irrevocable had taken charge which could neither be reversed nor halted, some mad scrambling of language and understanding which had already misjudged my naïve reasons for being here. I didn't realize then how normal it was for anyone, if put through the right preliminaries, to be swamped by guilt.

Since my sudden arrest and imprisonment, which at first I'd been ready to accept as some light charade touched with military confusion, I felt myself sinking, more and more, into the hands of some obscure accusation against which I ceased to look for an answer.

As the sun rose higher and whitened the rocks, the landscape turned blank, as though over-exposed. And with the whistling guards on each side of me, and the bully-shouldered officer up front, I was sure I was on the road to my doom. As my eyes grew used to the light – after all, I'd been two weeks in darkness – I saw the landscape shudder into shape, grow even more desolate and brutal. Yet never more precious as it floated past me, the worn-out skin of this irreplaceable world, marked here and there by the scribbled signs of man, a broken thatched cabin, or a terraced slope. Every breath I took now seemed rich and stolen, in spite of the oil-fumed heat in the car. Even the two armed guards, grotesque and scruffy as they were, began to take on the power and beauty of fates, protectors or destroyers, who held one's thread of life in their hands.

We'd been driving, I guessed, for about an hour, when the officer suddenly straightened up and snapped his fingers, and we pulled off the road and stopped. The dead icy tableland crept with yellow mist, and seemed quite empty save for a clump of trees in the distance. I was ordered out of the car, one of the guards stuck a gun in my back, pointed to the trees and said, 'March!'

Why had they brought me all this way, I wondered. They could have done the job more snugly back in the jail. Yet the place seemed apt and fitting enough; no doubt they'd used it before. The officer was out of the car now, coughing and spitting, and he came and gave my shoulder a light little shove. 'Come on, Rubio,' he said. 'Come on, march – let's go.' So I put up my head and marched . . .

I saw the vast cold sky and the stony plain and I began to walk towards the distant trees. I heard the soldiers behind me slip the bolts on their rifles. This then, of course, could be the chosen place – the plateau ringed by rock, the late dawn on our breath, the empty silence around us, the little wood ahead, all set for quiet execution or murder. I felt the sharp edges of the stones under my thin-soled shoes. The guards behind me shuttled the bolts of their guns.

If my moment was coming – and I now felt certain it was – I told myself not to look back. My intentions were simple. If they gave me enough time, and I was able to reach the little wood ahead of them, that would be my last chance – and I'd make a break for it. The nearest wind-bent tree looked a thousand years old, its roots pouring over the rocks like wax. The guards were snuffling behind me. Would I reach it before they fired? Would I hear the blast before the thumping bullets hit me? Would I hear anything before the dark? I walked slowly, almost mincingly, trying not to appear to hurry. I reached the trees and prepared to run . . .

One of the guards came up behind me and took my arm. 'OK, Rubio,' he said. 'Sit down.' His comrade was already squatting under a tree and opening a tin of sardines with his bayonet. The officer and driver joined us, yawning and scratching, and we sat down in a circle together. They gave me sardines and some bread, and passed round a bottle of coñac, and as I looked at the food in my hand, and at the raw, safe landscape around me, I was seized by a brief spasm of uncontrollable happiness.

The soldiers stretched out their legs and began talking about football. The officer brushed down his clothes and rolled me a cigarette. He waved his hand at the scenery, the old trees and the rocks, and said it was his favourite spot for a picnic. They came here, he said, about twice a week. I asked him where we were going now.

'To Figueras, of course,' he said. They were going to drop me off at the barracks. 'We thought you'd rather ride than walk.'

But he was still responsible for me, he said, if I liked to think of it that way. But only till they'd delivered me to Brigade Headquarters, then he'd be clear of me. He looked at me oddly with his hazed, blue eyes, slightly mad, amused yet cold.

Why hadn't he explained all this before? The car, the armed guards, the remote stop in the hills. Had this been another test, or some daft Spanish joke? Was he really as harmless as he appeared to be? Would he have been equally amused if I'd made that dash through the trees? There's no doubt what would have happened then.

PENGUIN 60s

ISABEL ALLENDE · *Voices in My Ear*
NICHOLSON BAKER · *Playing Trombone*
LINDSEY BAREHAM · *The Little Book of Big Soups*
KAREN BLIXEN · *From the Ngong Hills*
DIRK BOGARDE · *Coming of Age*
ANTHONY BURGESS · *Childhood*
ANGELA CARTER · *Lizzie Borden*
CARLOS CASTANEDA · *The Sorcerer's Ring of Power*
ELIZABETH DAVID · *Peperonata and Other Italian Dishes*
RICHARD DAWKINS · *The Pocket Watchmaker*
GERALD DURRELL · *The Pageant of Fireflies*
RICHARD ELLMANN · *The Trial of Oscar Wilde*
EPICURUS · *Letter on Happiness*
MARIANNE FAITHFULL · *Year One*
KEITH FLOYD · *Hot and Spicy Floyd*
ALEXANDER FRATER · *Where the Dawn Comes Up Like Thunder*
ESTHER FREUD · *Meeting Bilal*
JOHN KENNETH GALBRAITH · *The Culture of Contentment*
ROB GRANT AND DOUG NAYLOR · *Scenes from the Dwarf*
ROBERT GRAVES · *The Gods of Olympus*
JANE GRIGSON · *Puddings*
SOPHIE GRIGSON · *From Sophie's Table*
KATHARINE HEPBURN · *Little Me*
SUSAN HILL · *The Badness Within Him*
ALAN HOLLINGHURST · *Adventures Underground*
BARRY HUMPHRIES · *Less is More Please*
HOWARD JACOBSON · *Expulsion from Paradise*
P. D. JAMES · *The Girl Who Loved Graveyards*
STEPHEN KING · *Umney's Last Case*
LAO TZU · *Tao Te Ching*
DAVID LEAVITT · *Chips Is Here*

PENGUIN 60s

LAURIE LEE · *To War in Spain*
PATRICK LEIGH FERMOR · *Loose as the Wind*
ELMORE LEONARD · *Trouble at Rindo's Station*
DAVID LODGE · *Surprised by Summer*
BERNARD MAC LAVERTY · *The Miraculous Candidate*
SHENA MACKAY · *Cloud-Cuckoo-Land*
NORMAN MAILER · *The Dressing Room*
PETER MAYLE · *Postcards from Summer*
JAN MORRIS · *Scenes from Havian Life*
BLAKE MORRISON · *Camp Cuba*
VLADIMIR NABOKOV · *Now Remember*
REDMOND O'HANLON · *A River in Borneo*
STEVEN PINKER · *Thinking in Tongues*
CRAIG RAINE · *Private View*
CLAUDIA RODEN · *Ful Medames and Other Vegetarian Dishes*
HELGE RUBINSTEIN · *Chocolate Parfait*
SIMON SCHAMA · *The Taking of the Bastille*
WILL SELF · *The Rock of Crack As Big As the Ritz*
MARK SHAND · *Elephant Tales*
NIGEL SLATER · *30-Minute Suppers*
RICK STEIN · *Fresh from the Sea*
LYTTON STRACHEY · *Florence Nightingale*
PAUL THEROUX · *Slow Trains to Simla*
COLIN THUBRON · *Samarkand*
MARK TULLY · *Beyond Purdah*
LAURENS VAN DER POST · *Merry Christmas, Mr Lawrence*
MARGARET VISSER · *More than Meets the Eye*
GAVIN YOUNG · *Something of Samoa*

and

Thirty Obituaries from Wisden · SELECTED BY MATTHEW ENGEL

READ MORE IN PENGUIN

For complete information about books available from Penguin and how to order them, please write to us at the appropriate address below. Please note that for copyright reasons the selection of books varies from country to country.